David E Folsom, Nathaniel Pitt Langford

The Folsom-Cook Exploration of the Upper Yellowstone in the year 1869

David E Folsom, Nathaniel Pitt Langford

The Folsom-Cook Exploration of the Upper Yellowstone in the year 1869

ISBN/EAN: 9783744785037

Printed in Europe, USA, Canada, Australia, Japan

Cover: Foto ©Andreas Hilbeck / pixelio.de

More available books at **www.hansebooks.com**

THE

FOLSOM-COOK EXPLORATION

OF THE

UPPER YELLOWSTONE

IN THE YEAR 1869.

BY

DAVID E. FOLSOM.

WITH A PREFACE

BY

NATHANIEL P. LANGFORD.

ST. PAUL, MINN.

1894.

PREFACE.

Nature seemingly delights in surrounding her grandeur and magnificence with difficulty and danger. Her wonders are hidden away from the busy haunts of men, are discovered at long intervals of time, and only attain notoriety by constant warfare with incredulity and unbelief. The wonders of the Yellowstone National Park were first brought to the knowledge of the people of Montana by David E. Folsom and C. W. Cook. Mr. Folsom had often heard vague and uncertain rumors of the strange phenomena to be seen near the headwaters of the Yellowstone and Fire Hole rivers. He was told by an occasional trapper that the Indians, taking counsel of their superstitious fears, believed that region to be the abode of evil spirits, and in their nomadic journeyings carefully avoided all near approach to it. This story, gathering in volume and embellishment as it was circulated throughout the mining camps of Montana, so wrought upon his curiosity that in September, 1869, he and Mr. Cook made a partial exploration of the region to solve their doubts. Bewildered and astounded at the marvels they beheld, they were, on their return, unwilling to risk their reputations for veracity by a full recital of them to a small company whom their friends had assembled to hear the account of their explorations. Mr. Folsom, however, published a careful account of his expedition in the Chicago *Western Monthly* for July, 1870, and this, with such information as could be gleaned from him, led to the organization of the Washburn exploring expedition, of which I was a member. This expedition greatly extended the range of Mr. Folsom's discoveries, and the various accounts of its explorations written by Washburn, Hedges,

Trumbull and myself, and published in the Montana papers, the *Overland Monthly* and *Scribner's* (now *Century*) *Magazine*, with the additions made in 1871 by Professor Hayden, induced Congress, in March, 1872, to set apart the entire locality as a National Park.

The following is the roster of the Washburn expedition: Gen. H. D. Washburn, Samuel T. Hauser, Cornelius Hedges, W. C. Gillette, Walter Trumbull, Truman C. Everts, Benj. Stickney, Jacob Smith and N. P. Langford, all of Helena, Montana. Gen. Washburn, then surveyor-general of Montana, was selected as leader, and we became known as "the Washburn party." Lieut. Gustavus C. Doane, commanding five cavalrymen, accompanied the expedition.

Before we left Helena Mr. Folsom furnished us with a map showing his route of travel, and imparted to us much valuable information, and, as we afterwards learned, discussed with Gen. Washburn the project of creating a park, but I do not find that he ever published through the press his views on this subject.

Cornelius Hedges, of Helena, wrote the first articles ever published, urging the withdrawal of this region from private occupancy and dedicating it to the public as a park. I distinctly recall the place and the occasion when he first broached the subject to the members of our party. It was in the first camp we made after leaving the Lower Geyser Basin. We were seated round the camp-fire, and one of our number suggested that a quarter section of land opposite the great falls of the Yellowstone would be a source of profit to its owner. Another member of the party thought that the Upper Geyser Basin would furnish greater attractions for pleasure-seekers. Mr. Hedges then said that there ought to be no private ownership of any portion of that region, but that the whole of it ought to be set apart as a great national park. The suggestion met with a quick and favorable response from all the members of the party, and, to quote from a recent letter of Mr. Hedges to me, "the idea found favor with all, and from that time we never lost sight of it." On our return Mr. Hedges advocated the project in the public press. I have now in my possession a copy of the Helena *Herald* of Nov. 9, 1870, containing a letter of Mr. Hedges, in which he advocated the scheme; and in my lectures delivered in Washington and New York in January, 1871, I directed attention to Mr. Hedges' suggestions, and urged the passage by Congress of an act setting apart that region as a public park. All this was several months prior to any government exploration.

With an inspiration that ever asserted itself, and that frequently provoked the mirth and commiseration of my less enthusiastic friends, I preserved nearly all the newspaper and magazine articles written by my comrades-in-arms; and upon the question now so frequently asked, "Who first originated the idea of the National Park?" these old letters, lectures and records return a verdict which is not an afterthought, and which is at once inexorable and unassailable.

Hon. Wm. H. Clagett, delegate from Montana, drew the park bill and gave a copy to Senator Pomeroy, chairman of the senate committee on public lands, who introduced it in the senate; and while both of these gentlemen and Hon. Mark Dunnell and Prof. Hayden and myself did hard work in Washington for the passage of the act of dedication, no person can divide with Messrs. Hedges and Folsom the honor of *originating the idea* of creating the Yellowstone National Park.

I cannot forbear, *en passant*, emphasizing the importance of correcting, as far as is possible, at this early day in the history of the Park, all popular errors concerning it. Traditions and legends, repeated through a long series of years, come at last to be accepted as unquestioned facts of history. In one of the Park guide books containing information for tourists I find the following:

"The earliest reference to the hot springs is in the stories of a trapper by the name of Colter, who accompanied Lewis and Clark's celebrated expedition across the continent. On the return of this expedition, when below the mouth of the Yellowstone, Colter was discharged at his own request, and immediately returned to the country above the forks of the Missouri. In this neighborhood, probably on the Jefferson, his companion, Potts, was killed by the Blackfeet and he was captured. Almost miraculously he escaped from them, and, entirely naked, made his way to a trading post on the Big Horn. After this he lived for a year or more among the Bannacks, whose range included what is now the Yellowstone Park. Either during his perilous journey after his escape from the Blackfeet, or during his sojourn among the Bannacks, he became acquainted with the region of the hot springs and geysers, for we find him in Missouri in 1810, telling marvelous tales of lakes of burning pitch, of land on fire, hot springs and geysers. His stories were, of course, treated as travelers' tales, and 'Colter's Hell' was classed with Lilliput, Symmes' Hole and other inventions of over-developed imaginations.''

While the foregoing may be *literally* correct, it is misleading. It gives the reader the impression that Colter visited the Fire Hole river, and that the Fire Hole valley and "Colter's Hell" are identical, but I do not know of any facts that warrant this belief. Colter severed his connection with the Lewis and Clark expedition just below the mouth of the Yellowstone on August 15, 1806. Under date of August 14, 1806, the Lewis and Clark journal reads:

"Colter * * * was desirous of joining the two trappers who had accompanied us, and who now proposed an expedition up the river in which they were to find traps and give him a share of the profits, * * * and he left us the next day.''

We do not know where Colter spent the following winter (1806-7), but he probably wintered on the lower Yellowstone, for in 1807 he was on Pryor's Fork of that river. On one of the Lewis and Clark maps, published in 1814 in the Paul Allen edition of their report, Colter's route of travel is distinctly marked by dotted lines. From Pryor's Fork he moved westward to the Yellowstone which he crossed just below the Grand Cañon. He then followed up the river on the west side, passing by Crater Hills and Sulphur Mountain, thence along the west shore of Yellowstone lake, rounding the southwesterly arm to the south side, and thence crossed the dividing ridge of the Rocky mountains to the river or creek which bears his name, and which was supposed to be one of the forming streams of the Rio del Norte, but which afterwards proved to be a tributary of Snake river. His route, so plainly marked on the map, does not indicate that he crossed the divide between the Yellowstone and Fire Hole rivers.

On the second map published with Dr. Elliott Coues' edition of Lewis and Clark's journal, "Colter's Hell" is located on the Stinkingwater branch of the Big Horn, near the northern boundary of Wyoming, and one hundred and ten miles east of the upper geyser basin. If there are to be found no hot springs in that locality at the present time, this fact is no evidence that there were none in 1810. Among the marvels of the Yellowstone none are more wonderful than the powers of reproduction and the elements of rapid decay and destruction everywhere to be seen. Large springs, which on my first visit in 1870 were boiling, were quiescent and nearly cold when I was there in 1872. The immense mud volcano, described in 1870 by Washburn and Hedges as one of the most wonderful features of that region, and down the outer rim of the crater of which Mr. Hedges was thrown by the explosive force of the steam (vide Gen. Washburn's letter), had nearly disappeared two years later, leaving nothing but a shapeless and unsightly hole three times the size of the former crater, in which large tree tops were swaying to and fro in the gurgling mass of mud fifty feet below, the whole appearance bearing testimony to the terrible nature of the convulsion which wrought such destruction. Causes which in that region are so unnaturally natural, and are at war with all experiences elsewhere, have long ago extinguished the fires of "Colter's Hell."

No words can magnify the wonders of this natural pleasuring ground. Nowhere in the same limits has Nature crowded so much of grandeur and majesty with so much of novelty and wonder. In the catalogue of earthly wonders this is the greatest. It confers a distinctive character upon our country;—and next to these marvels themselves, nothing will be of greater interest to the thousands who through all coming time will visit this region, than a true history of the explorations of the men who first penetrated into those far off recesses of the mountains, and who brought to the notice of the world these marvels which had existed so long in impenetrable seclusion and almost inaccessible to human approach. We trace the creation of the park from the Folsom-Cook expedition of 1869 to the Washburn expedition of 1870, and thence to the Hayden expedition (U. S. Geological Survey) of 1871. Not to one of these expeditions more than to another do we owe the legislation which set apart this "pleasuring-ground for the benefit and enjoyment of the people."

The office of the *Western Monthly*, of Chicago, was destroyed by fire soon after the publication of Mr. Folsom's account of his discoveries, and the only copy of that magazine which he possessed, and which he presented to the Historical Society of Montana, met a like fate in the great Helena fire. The copy which I possess is perhaps the only one to be found.

A quarter of a century has passed since that exploration was made. The ranks of the old settlers of Montana are being rapidly thinned. Few remain of those who welcomed the safe return from their perilous journey of these first explorers, and listened to a recital of their adventures. For the purpose of preserving the history of the initial step which eventuated in giving to the American people the Yellowstone National Park, and to the end that the truth may be established in the mouth of two or three living witnesses, the report of Mr. Folsom is here re-published.

NATHANIEL P. LANGFORD.

St. Paul, Minn., June 16, 1894.

THE VALLEY OF THE UPPER YELLOWSTONE.

BY DAVID E. FOLSOM.

THE country around the headwaters of the Yellowstone river, although frequently visited by prospectors and mountain men, is still to the world of letters a veritable *terra incognita.* Environed by mountain chains that are covered by a dense growth of timber, making all approaches to it seem difficult, it has no regularly traveled route, and no party of emigrants on their way to the Pacific slope has ever passed through it; nor has any expedition under the patronage of the Government yet attempted to penetrate its fastnesses. The hardy prospectors, searching in this region for new "diggings," have hitherto failed to find gold in paying quantities; but have always returned to repeat the tales of wonderful waterfalls a thousand feet in height, of innumerable hot springs of surprising magnitude, and of vast tracts of country covered with the *scoria* of volcanoes—some of which were reported to be in active operation. Owing to the fact that this class of men had gained a reputation for indulging in flights of fancy when recounting their adventures, these reports were received with considerable incredulity until it was noticed that, however much the accounts of different parties differed in detail, there was a marked coincidence in the descriptions of some of the most prominent features of the country.

In 1867, an exploring expedition from Virginia City, Montana Territory, was talked of, but for some unknown reason—probably for the want of a sufficient number to engage in it—it was abandoned. The next year another was planned, which ended like the first—in talk. Early in the summer of 1869, the newspapers throughout the Territory announced that a party of citizens from Helena, Virginia City and Bozeman, accompanied by some of the officers stationed at Fort Ellis, with an escort of soldiers, would leave Bozeman about the fifth of September, for the Yellowstone country, with the intention of making a thorough examination of all the wonders with which that region was said to abound. The party was expected to be limited in numbers, and to be composed of some of the most prominent men in the Territory, and the writer felt extremely flattered when his earnest request to have his name added to the list was granted. He joined with two personal friends in getting an outfit, and then waited patiently for the other members of the party to perfect their arrangements. About a month before the day fixed for starting, some of the members began to discover that pressing business engagements would prevent their going. Then came news from Fort Ellis that, owing to some changes made in the disposition of troops stationed in the Territory, the military portion of the party would be unable to join the expedition; and our party, which had now dwindled down to ten or twelve persons, thinking it would be unsafe for so small a number to venture where there was a strong probability of meeting with hostile Indians, also abandoned the undertaking. But the writer and his two friends before mentioned, believing that the dangers to be encountered had been magnified, and trusting by vigilance and good luck to avoid them, resolved to attempt the journey at all hazards.

We provided ourselves with five horses—three of them for the saddle, and the other two for carrying our cooking utensils, ammunition, fishing tackle, blankets and buffalo robes, a pick and pan, a shovel, an axe, and provisions necessary for a six weeks' trip. We were all well armed with repeating rifles, Colt's six-shooters and sheath-knives, and had besides a double-barrelled shot-gun for small game. We also had a good field-glass, a pocket compass and a thermometer.

On the sixth of September we started from Diamond City —a mining town on a small tributary of the Missouri river, forty miles east of Helena. Our second day's journey brought us to Gallatin City, at the "three forks" of the Missouri. From Gallatin City a ride of three hours brought us to Hamilton—a post town situated near the centre of the Gallatin valley—where we camped for the night. From Hamilton to Bozeman, a distance of eighteen miles, our route lay through a beautiful farming country, where generous stacks of grain, or wide fields covered with golden sheaves, indicated the propriety of calling this valley the Genesee of Montana. Bozeman is a thriving frontier town, pleasantly located in the eastern part of the Gallatin valley. Bozeman Pass—the lowest pass in the divide between the waters of the Yellowstone and the Missouri rivers—has been surveyed as the proposed route for the Northern Pacific Railroad.

Two and one-half miles from Bozeman we passed Fort Ellis, soon after leaving which we took a trail leading up a creek which is one of the tributaries of the East Gallatin, and in a short time found ourselves traversing a deep ravine, bounded on the left by a perpendicular wall of limestone a thousand feet in height, while on the right the mountains rose in irregular steps or terraces, covered with a dense growth of spruce. In some places the mass of dark green foliage was unbroken from base to summit; at others it was relieved by beetling cliffs of fantastic shape, so characteristic of the limestone formation. On one of the highest points stood a huge rock that bore a strong resemblance to an old castle; rampart and bulwark were slowly yielding to the ravages of time, but the stout old turret stood out in bold relief against the sky, with every embrasure as perfect in outline as though but a day ago it had been built by the hand of man. We could almost imagine that it was the stronghold of some baron of feudal times, and that we were his retainers returning laden with the spoils of a successful foray. As we approached the summit the timber appeared only in patches, and the hills on either hand were less abrupt, and covered with a luxuriant growth of bunch-grass, which affords fine pasturage for the numerous herds of antelope which roam there. Immediately after crossing the divide we struck the head of Trail creek and followed it down six or seven miles in an easterly direction to where it debouched from the foot-hills into the valley of the Yel-lowstone. Here we turned in a southerly direction, over a low rolling plateau covered with prickly pear, through which our horses gingerly picked their way, and arrived at the river about sunset. This valley is about twenty-five miles long, and varies in width from one to five miles; at the foot of it the mountains close in on both sides, forming a cañon, below which is the Yellowstone valley proper.

We pushed on up the valley, following the general course of the river as well as we could, but frequently making short *detours* through the foot-hills to avoid the deep ravines and places where the hills terminated abruptly at the water's edge. On the eighth day out we encountered a band of In-dians, who, however, proved to be Tonkeys, or Sheepeaters, and friendly. The discovery of their character relieved our minds of apprehension, and we conversed with them as well as their limited knowledge of English and ours of panto-mime would permit. For several hours after leaving them we traveled over a high, rolling table-land, diversified by sparkling lakes, picturesque rocks and beautiful groves of timber. Two or three miles to our left we could see the deep gorge which the river, flowing westward, had cut through the mountains. The river soon after resumed its northern course, and from this point to the falls, a distance of twenty-five or thirty miles, it is believed to flow through one continuous cañon, through which no one has ever been able to pass.

At this point we left the main river, intending to follow up the east branch for one day, then to turn in a southwest course and endeavor to strike the river again near the falls. After going a short distance we encountered a cañon about three miles in length, and while passing around it we caught a glimpse of scenery so grand and striking that we decided to stop for a day or two and give it a more extended examination. We picked our way to a timbered point about mid-way of the cañon, and found ourselves upon the verge of an overhanging cliff at least seven hundred feet in height. The opposite bluff was about on a level with the place where we were standing, and it maintained this height for a mile up the river, but gradually sloped away toward the foot of the cañon. The upper half presented an unbroken face, with here and there a re-entering angle, but everywhere maintained its perpendicularity; the lower half was composed of the *debris* that had fallen from the wall. But the most singular feature was the formation of the perpendicular wall. At the top there was a stratum of basalt, from thirty to forty feet thick, standing in hexagonal columns; beneath that, a bed of conglomerate eighty feet thick, composed of washed gravel and boulders; then another stratum of columnar basalt of about half the thickness of the first; and, lastly, what appeared to be a bed of coarse sandstone. A short distance above us, rising from the bed of the river, stood a monument or pyramid of conglomerate, circular in form, which we estimated to be forty feet in diameter at the base and three hundred feet high, diminishing in size in a true taper to its top, which was not more than three feet across. It was so slender that it looked as if one man could topple it over. How it was formed I leave others to conjecture. We could see the river for nearly the whole distance through the cañon—now dashing over some miniature cataract, now fretting against huge boulders that seemed to have been hurled by some giant hand to stay its progress, and anon circling in quiet eddies beneath the dark shadows of some projecting rock. The water was so transparent that we could see the bottom from where we were standing, and it had that peculiar liquid emerald tinge so characteristic of our mountain streams.

Half a mile down the river, and near the foot of the bluff,
was a chalky looking bank, from which steam and smoke
were rising, and on repairing to the spot we found a vast
number of hot sulphur springs. The steam was issuing
from every crevice and hole in the rocks, and, being highly
impregnated with sulphur, it threw off sulphuretted hydrogen, making a stench that was very unpleasant. All the
crevices were lined with beautiful crystals of sulphur, as
delicate as frost-work. At some former period, not far distant, there must have been a volcanic eruption here. Much
of the *scoria* and ashes which were then thrown out has
been carried off by the river, but enough still remains to
form a bar seventy-five or a hundred feet in depth. Smoke
was still issuing from the rocks in one place, from which a
considerable amount of lava had been discharged within a
few days or weeks at farthest. While we were standing by,
several gallons of a black liquid ran down and hardened
upon the rocks. We broke some of this off and brought it
away, and it proved to be sulphur, pure enough to burn
readily when ignited.

September 18th—the twelfth day out—we found that ice
had formed one-fourth of an inch thick during the night,
and six inches of snow had fallen. The situation began to
look a little disagreeable, but the next day was bright and
clear, with promise of warm weather again in a few days.
Resuming our journey, we soon saw the serrated peaks of
the Big Horn range glistening like burnished silver in the
sunlight, and, overtowering them in the dim distance, the
Wind River mountains seemed to blend with the few fleecy
clouds that skirted their tops, while in the opposite direction, in contrast to the barren snow-capped peaks behind
us, as far as the eye could reach, mountain and valley were
covered with timber, whose dark green foliage deepened in
hue as it receded, till it terminated at the horizon in a bound-

less black forest. Taking our bearings as well as we could, we shaped our course in the direction in which we supposed the falls to be.

The next day (September 20th), we came to a gentle declivity at the head of a shallow ravine, from which steam rose in a hundred columns and united in a cloud so dense as to obscure the sun. In some places it spurted from the rocks in jets not larger than a pipe-stem; in others it curled gracefully up from the surface of boiling pools from five to fifteen feet in diameter. In some springs the water was clear and transparent; others contained so much sulphur that they looked like pots of boiling yellow paint. One of the largest was as black as ink. Near this was a fissure in the rocks several rods long and two feet across in the widest place at the surface, but enlarging as it descended. We could not see down to any great depth on account of the steam, but the ground echoed beneath our tread with a hollow sound, and we could hear the waters surging below, sending up a dull, resonant roar like the break of the ocean surf into a cave. At these springs but little water was discharged at the surface, it seeming to pass off by some subterranean passage. About half a mile down the ravine the springs broke out again. Here they were in groups, spreading out over several acres of ground. One of these groups —a collection of mud springs of various colors, situated one above the other on the left slope of the ravine—we christened "The Chemical Works." The mud, as it was discharged from the lower side, gave each spring the form of a basin or pool. At the bottom of the slope was a vat, ten by thirty feet, where all the ingredients from the springs above were united in a greenish-yellow compound of the consistency of white lead. Three miles further on we found more hot springs along the sides of a deep ravine, at the bottom of which flowed a creek twenty feet wide. Near the bank of the creek, through an aperture four inches in diameter, a column of steam rushed with a deafening roar, with such force that it maintained its size for forty feet in the air, then spread out and rolled away in a great cloud toward the heavens. We found here inexhaustible beds of sulphur and saltpetre. Alum was also abundant; a small pond in the vicinity, some three hundred yards long and half as wide, contained as much alum as it could hold in solution, and the mud along the shore was white with the same substance, crystallized by evaporation.

On September 21st, a pleasant ride of eighteen miles over an undulating country brought us to the great cañon, two miles below the falls, but there being no grass convenient, we passed on up the river to a point half a mile above the upper falls, and camped on a narrow flat close to the river bank. We spent the next day at the falls—a day that was a succession of surprises; and we returned to camp realizing, as we had never done before, how utterly insignificant are man's mightiest efforts when compared with the fulfilment of Omnipotent will. Language is entirely inadequate to convey a just conception of the awful grandeur and sublimity of this masterpiece of nature's handiwork, and in my brief description I shall confine myself to bare facts. Above our camp the river is about one hundred and fifty yards wide, and glides smoothly along between gently sloping banks, but just below the hills crowd in on either side, forcing the water into a narrow channel, through which it hurries with increasing speed, until, rushing through a *chute* sixty feet wide, it falls in an unbroken sheet over a precipice one hundred and fifteen feet in height. It widens out again, flows with steady course for half a mile between steep timbered bluffs four hundred feet high, and again narrowing in till it is not more than seventy-five feet wide, it makes the final fearful leap of three hundred and fifty feet. The ragged edges of the precipice tear the water into a thousand streams —all united together and yet apparently separate—changing it to the appearance of molten silver; the outer ones decrease in size as they increase in velocity, curl outward, and break into mist long before they reach the bottom. This cloud of mist conceals the river for two hundred yards, but it dashes out from beneath the rainbow-arch that spans the chasm, and thence, rushing over a succession of rapids and cascades, it vanishes at last where a sudden turn of the river seems to bring the two walls of the cañon together. Below the falls the hills gradually increase in height for two miles, where they assume the proportions of mountains. Here the cañon is at least fifteen hundred feet deep, with an average width of twice that distance at the top. For one-third of the distance downwards, the sides are perpendicular, from thence running down to the river in steep ridges crowned by rocks of the most grotesque form and color, and it required no stretch of the imagination to picture fortresses, castles, watch-towers and other ancient struct-ures of every conceivable shape. In several places near the bottom, steam issued from the rocks, and, judging from the indications, there were at some former period hot springs or steam jets of immense size all along the wall.

The next day we resumed our journey, traversing the northern slope of a high plateau between the Yellowstone and Snake rivers. Unlike the dashing mountain stream we had thus far followed, the Yellowstone was in this part of its course wide and deep, flowing with a gentle current along the foot of low hills or meandering in graceful curves through broad and grassy meadows. Some twelve miles from the falls we came to a collection of hot springs that deserve more than a passing notice. These, like the most we saw, were situated upon a hill-side, and as we ap-proached them we could see the steam rising in puffs at reg-ular intervals of fifteen or twenty seconds, accompanied by dull explosions which could be heard half a mile away, sounding like the discharge of a blast underground. These explosions came from a large cave that ran back under the hill, from which mud had been discharged in such quantities as to form a heavy embankment twenty feet higher than the floor of the cave, which prevented the mud from flowing off, but the escaping steam had kept a hole, some twenty feet in diameter, open up through the mud in front of the entrance to the cave. The cave seemed nearly filled with mud, and the steam rushed out with such volume and force as to lift the whole mass up against the roof and dash it out into the open space in front, and then, as the cloud of steam lifted, we could see the mud settling back in turbid waves into the cavern again. Three hundred yards from the mud cave was another that discharged pure water; the entrance to it was in the form of a perfect arch, seven feet in height and five in width. A short distance below these caves were several large sulphur springs, the most remarkable of which was a shallow pool seventy-five feet in diameter, in which clear water on one side and yellow mud on the other were gently boiling without mingling.

September 24th we arrived at Yellowstone Lake, about twenty miles from the falls. The main body of this beautiful sheet of water is ten miles wide from east to west, and sixteen miles long from north to south, but at the south end it puts out two arms, one to the southeast and the other to the southwest, making the entire length of the lake about thirty miles. Its shores—whether gently sloping mountains, bold promontories, low necks or level prairies—are everywhere covered with timber. The lake has three small islands, which are also heavily timbered. The outlet is at the northwest extremity. The lake abounds with trout, and the shallow water in its coves affords feeding ground for thousands of wild ducks, geese, pelicans and swans.

We ascended to the head of the lake and remained in its vicinity for several days, resting ourselves and our horses, and viewing the many objects of interest and wonder. Among these were springs differing from any we had previously seen. They were situated along the shore for a distance of two miles, extending back from it about five hundred yards and into the lake perhaps as many feet. The ground in many places gradually sloped down to the water's edge, while in others the white chalky cliffs rose fifteen feet high, the waves having worn the rock away at the base, leaving the upper portion projecting over in some places twenty feet. There were several hundred springs here, varying in size from miniature fountains to pools or wells seventy-five feet in diameter and of great depth. The water had a pale violet tinge, and was very clear, enabling us to discern small objects fifty or sixty feet below the surface. In some of these, vast openings led off at the side, and as the slanting rays of the sun lit up these deep caverns we could see the rocks hanging from their roofs, their water-worn sides and rocky floors, almost as plainly as if we had been traversing their silent chambers. These springs were intermittent, flowing or boiling at irregular intervals. The greater portion of them were perfectly quiet while we were there, although nearly all gave unmistakable evidence of frequent activity. Some of them would quietly settle for ten feet, while another would as quietly rise until it overflowed its banks, and send a torrent of hot water sweeping down to the lake. At the same time, one near at hand would send up a sparkling jet of water ten or twelve feet high, which would fall back into its basin, and then perhaps instantly stop boiling and quietly settle into the earth, or suddenly rise and discharge its waters in every direction over the rim; while another, as if wishing to attract our wondering gaze, would throw up a cone six feet in diameter and eight feet high, with a loud roar. These changes, each one of which would possess some new feature, were constantly going on; sometimes they would occur within the space of a few minutes, and again hours would elapse before any change could be noted. At the water's edge, along the lake shore, there were several mounds of solid stone, on the top of each of which was a small basin with a perforated bottom. These also overflowed at times, and the hot water trickled down on every side. Thus, by the slow process of precipitation, through the countless lapse of ages, these stone monuments have been formed. A small cluster of mud springs near by claimed our attention. They were like hollow truncated cones and oblong mounds, three or four feet in height. These were filled with mud, resembling thick paint of the finest quality, differing in color from pure white to the various shades of yellow, pink, red and violet. Some of these boiling pots were less than a foot in diameter. The mud in them would slowly rise and fall, as the bubbles of escaping steam, following one after the other, would burst upon the surface. During the afternoon they threw mud to the height of fifteen feet for a few minutes, and then settled back to their former quietude.

As we were about departing on our homeward trip we ascended the summit of a neighboring hill and took a final look at Yellowstone Lake. Nestled among the forest-crowned hills which bounded our vision, lay this inland sea, its crystal waves dancing and sparkling in the sunlight as if laughing with joy for their wild freedom. It is a scene of transcendant beauty which has been viewed by but few white men, and we felt glad to have looked upon it before its primeval solitude should be broken by the crowds of pleasure seekers which at no distant day will throng its shores.

September 29th we took up our march for home. Our plan was to cross the range in a northwesterly direction, find the Madison river, and follow it down to civilization. Twelve miles brought us to a small triangular-shaped lake, about eight miles long, deeply set among the hills. We kept on in a northwesterly direction as near as the rugged nature of the country would permit, and on the third day (October 1st) came to a small irregularly shaped valley, some six miles across in the widest place, from every part of which great clouds of steam arose. From descriptions which we had had of this valley from persons who had previously visited it, we recognized it as the place known as

"Burnt Hole," or "Death Valley." The Madison river flows through it, and from the general contour of the country we knew that it headed in the lake which we passed two days ago, only twelve miles from the Yellowstone. We descended into the valley and found that the springs had the same general characteristics as those I have already described, although some of them were much larger and discharged a vast amount of water. One of them, at a little distance, attracted our attention by the immense amount of steam it threw off, and upon approaching it we found it to be an intermittent geyser in active operation. The hole through which the water was discharged was ten feet in diameter, and was situated in the centre of a large circular shallow basin, into which the water fell. There was a stiff breeze blowing at the time, and by going to the windward side and carefully picking our way over convenient stones, we were enabled to reach the edge of the hole. At that moment the escaping steam was causing the water to boil up in a fountain five or six feet high. It stopped in an instant, and commenced settling down—twenty, thirty, forty feet—until we concluded that the bottom had fallen out, but the next instant, without any warning, it came rushing up and shot into the air at least eighty feet, causing us to stampede for higher ground. It continued to spout at intervals of a few minutes for some time, but finally subsided, and was quiet during the remainder of the time we stayed in the vicinity. We followed up the Madison five miles, and there found the most gigantic hot springs we had seen. They were situated along the river bank, and discharged so much hot water that the river was blood warm a quarter of a mile below. One of the springs was two hundred and fifty feet in diameter, and had every indication of spouting powerfully at times. The waters from the hot springs in this valley, if united, would form a large stream, and they increase the size of the river nearly one-half. Although we experienced no bad effects from passing through the "Val-

ley of Death," yet we were not disposed to dispute the propriety of giving it that name. It seemed to be shunned by
all animated nature. There were no fish in the river, no
birds in the trees, no animals—not even a track—anywhere
to be seen, although in one spring we saw the entire skele-
ton of a buffalo that had probably fallen in accidentally and
been boiled down to soup.

Leaving this remarkable valley, we followed the course of
the Madison, sometimes through level valleys, and sometimes through deep cuts in mountain ranges, and on the
fourth of October emerged from a cañon, ten miles long and
with high and precipitous mountain sides, to find the broad
valley of the Lower Madison spread out before us. Here
we could recognize familiar landmarks in some of the mountain peaks around Virginia City. From this point we com-
pleted our journey by easy stages, and arrived at home on
the evening of the eleventh. We had been absent thirty-six
days—a much longer time than our friends had anticipated
—and we found that they were seriously contemplating or-
ganizing a party to go in search of us.

www.ingramcontent.com/pod-product-compliance
Lightning Source LLC
Chambersburg PA
CBHW031157090426
42738CB00008B/1376